D1523513

Americans at War

TIMELINE *of* WORLD WAR II EUROPE & NORTH AFRICA

By Charlie Samuels

Gareth Stevens
Publishing

Please visit our website, www.garethstevens.com. For a free color catalog of all our high-quality books, call toll free 1-800-542-2595 or fax 1-877-542-2596.

Library of Congress Cataloging-in-Publication Data
Samuels, Charlie, 1961-
 Timeline of World War II. Europe and North Africa / Charlie Samuels.
    p. cm. — (Americans at war : a Gareth Stevens timeline series)
 Includes bibliographical references and index.
 ISBN 978-1-4339-5932-5 (pbk.)
 ISBN 978-1-4339-5933-2 (6-pack)
 ISBN 978-1-4339-5930-1 (library binding)
 1. World War, 1939-1945—Campaigns—Europe—Juvenile literature. 2. World War, 1939-1945—Campaigns—Africa, North—Juvenile literature. 3. World War, 1939-1945—Campaigns—Europe—Chronology—Juvenile literature. 4. World War, 1939-1945—Campaigns—Africa, North—Chronology—Juvenile literature. I. Title. II. Title: Timeline of World War 2. Europe and North Africa. III. Title: Timeline of World War Two. Europe and North Africa.
 D756.S225 2011
 940.54'21—dc22

                                                                        2010049254

Published in 2012 by
Gareth Stevens Publishing
111 East 14th Street, Suite 349
New York, NY 10003

© 2011 Brown Bear Books Ltd

For Brown Bear Books Ltd:
Editorial Director: Lindsey Lowe
Managing Editor: Tim Cooke
Children's Publisher: Anne O'Daly
Art Director: Jeni Child
Designer: Karen Perry
Picture Manager: Sophie Mortimer
Production Director: Alastair Gourlay

Picture Credits:
Front Cover: Robert Hunt Library

Key: t = top, b = bottom
AKG Images: 11, 19b, 20; **Lebrecht Collection:** 10, 13, 16, 30, 36; **Nik Cornish:** 23, 35b, 37t, 37b; **Robert Hunt Library:** 6, 7, 8t, 8b, 9, 12, 14, 15t, 17, 19t, 21t, 22, 25, 26, 27, 28, 29, 31, 32t, 32b, 34, 38, 39, 40t, 40b, 41, 42, 43, 44t, 44b, 45; **TopFoto:** 15b, 18, 24, 35t, 21b

All Artworks © Brown Bear Books Ltd

Publisher's note to educators and parents: Our editors have carefully reviewed the websites that appear on p. 47 to ensure that they are suitable for students. Many websites change frequently, however, and we cannot guarantee that a site's future contents will continue to meet our high standards of quality and educational value. Be advised that students should be closely supervised whenever they access the Internet.

Manufactured in the United States of America
1 2 3 4 5 6 7 8 9 12 11 10

CPSIA compliance information: Batch #BRS11GS: For further information contact Gareth Stevens, New York, New York at 1-800-542-2595.

Contents

Introduction

World War II was the largest and most destructive war in history. Between 1939 and 1945, 100 million troops were mobilized across the world.

As many as 60 million people died in the conflict. Most were civilians who died as a result of bombing, starvation, disease, or persecution by brutal regimes. The biggest crime against civilians was the murder of six million Jews by the Nazis.

The Course of the War

Adolf Hitler's Nazi Party came to power in Germany in 1933 promising territorial expansion. Hitler's invasion of Poland on September 1, 1939, brought declarations of war from France and from Britain and its empire. Using a tactic known as blitzkrieg (lightning war), the Germans soon conquered much of Europe, dragging most of the continent into the war.

In June 1941 Hitler invaded the Soviet Union. Later that year, the United States entered the war after Germany's ally, Japan, bombed the US Pacific base at Pearl Harbor. The Allies agreed to prioritize the war in Europe and planned a landing in northern France that eventually took place in June 1944. Meanwhile, British and US troops had defeated the Axis in North Africa and advanced up the Italian peninsula; the Soviet Red Army had turned back the Germans and was heading west. The two fronts closed on Berlin, where Hitler shot himself amid the ruins of his empire shortly before Germany surrendered.

About This Book

This book focuses on the war in Europe and North Africa from 1939 to 1945. It contains two types of timelines. Along the bottom of the pages is a timeline that covers the whole period. It lists key events and developments, including from the Pacific War, color coded. Each chapter also has its own timeline, which runs vertically down the sides of the pages. This timeline gives more specific details about the particular subject of the chapter.

A convoy of Allied merchant ships crosses the Atlantic Ocean. Ships traveled together so they were easier to protect from German U-boats. ↓

Causes of the War

As Hitler's position grew more secure within Germany,
he began a campaign of territorial expansion that would
eventually lead Europe to war.

German troops →
remove a barrier at
a border crossing as
they invade Poland
on September 1, 1939.

Timeline
1939
January–
June

January 26 Spain Nationalists
capture Barcelona, which is the
Republican-held capital of Catalonia.

January   February   March

KEY:

 Politics

Land war

Sea and air war

March 10 Czechoslovakia Hitler begins the
takeover of Bohemia and Moravia, which are home
to many Germans. The operation concludes by
March 16; Czechoslovakia no longer exists.

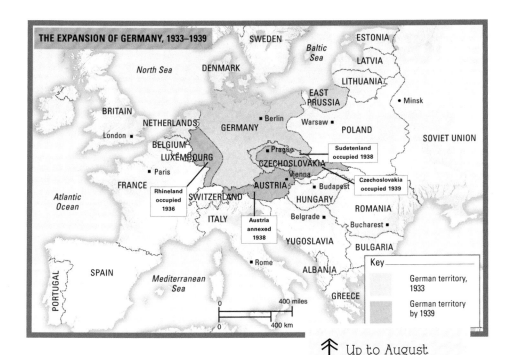

THE EXPANSION OF GERMANY, 1933–1939

Key

German territory, 1933

German territory by 1939

↑ Up to August 1939, Hitler expanded Germany while Europe watched.

Timeline

March 1938 Anschluss ("Union") between Germany and Austria.

September 1938 The Munich Conference agrees to Germany's occupation of the Sudetenland.

March 1939 Hitler occupies the rest of Czechoslovakia.

May 1939 Germany and Italy form the "Pact of Steel."

August 1939 Germany signs a nonaggression pact with the Soviet Union.

September 1, 1939 German forces invade Poland.

September 3, 1939 Britain, France, and their allies declare war on Germany.

Adolf Hitler came to power in Germany in 1933 saying he would reject what Germans saw as the unfair peace treaties that ended World War I in 1918. Hitler was determined to expand Germany to include the large German populations living in other countries. He rearmed Germany and occupied the Rhineland. Hitler's move was a gamble, but the neighboring French did nothing. They were waiting for support from Britain. The British, however, were suspicious of France's alliance with the Soviet Union.

← With no support, Czech president Benes had to give in to Hitler's demands.

May 22 Italy The Italian government forges stronger ties with Germany in an alliance known as the "Pact of Steel."

April   May   June

March 28 Spain Nationalist troops enter Madrid, marking the end of a civil war in which 300,000 Spaniards have died; General Francisco Franco takes over the government.

Munich Conference

British prime minister Neville Chamberlain called a conference in Munich to try to avoid war. He thought that if the Allies gave in to Hitler's demands for the return of "German" lands, Hitler would not go to war. But Hitler saw "appeasement" as a sign of weakness and proof that the Allies would not intervene if he went to war.

German troops enter the Rhineland on March 7, 1936. ⟹

Mussolini and Hitler, at left, face Chamberlain (far right) in Munich in September 1938.

Hitler and Mussolini

In October 1936, Italian dictator Benito Mussolini and Hitler formed the Rome–Berlin Axis. Italy's support allowed Hitler to declare Austria a province of the German Reich, or empire, in March 1938.

The democracies' failure to act encouraged Hitler to target the Sudetenland, a Czech border area with many Germans. At an international conference at Munich in September 1938, Hitler got his way (see box left): The Czechs were told to leave the Sudetenland. Hitler

Timeline
1939
July–
December

August 23 Germany The Nazi government signs a nonaggression pact with the Soviet Union. The Soviets will allow Germany to invade Poland; in return, Germany will divide Poland with the Soviet Union.

September 1 Poland A large German force invades; with few tanks or aircraft, Poland is quickly overwhelmed.

July   August   September

September 3 Europe Britain, France, Australia, and New Zealand declare war on Nazi Germany.

KEY:

Politics

Land war

Sea and air war

now believed that neither Britain nor France would fight. In March 1939, his troops occupied the rest of Czechoslovakia.

The Polish Question

Hitler turned to Poland, which included two areas that were home to about a million Germans. In order to avoid a possible alliance of Britain, France, and the Soviet Union, Hitler made a pact with Stalin's Soviet Union (see box, right). The western democracies decided to make a stand, however. Britain and France offered to guarantee Polish independence.

On August 31, SS troops in Polish uniforms staged a mock raid on a radio station in the German border town of Gleiwitz. Hitler used the "raid" as an excuse to invade Poland on September 1, 1939. Two days later, France and Britain declared war on Germany, as did Britain's dependencies. World War II had begun.

↑ Germans in Sudetenland salute as German troops enter Friedland on October 3, 1938.

Hitler and Stalin

The failure of France and Britain to halt Hitler's demands at Munich had had an important effect on Soviet leader Joseph Stalin. He decided he had to cope with German expansion eastward without their help. In August 1939, Stalin signed a nonaggression pact with Germany, which included a deal to divide Poland between them in the event of war. The agreement between fascism on one side and communism on the other shocked the world. It also left Hitler with a free hand in Poland.

September 18–30 Poland Poland is defeated and split into German and Soviet zones of occupation; many Poles escape.

November 30 Finland Some 600,000 Soviet troops invade Finland. Despite inferior numbers, the Finns hold the invaders at the Mannerheim Line. Soviet troops struggle because they have no winter clothes.

October   November   December

October 14 North Sea A U-boat (submarine) sinks the battleship HMS *Royal Oak* in the British base at Scapa Flow, with the loss of 786 lives.

December 13 Atlantic Ocean The British trap the German pocket battleship *Graf Spee* at the mouth of the River Plate, Uruguay; the damaged ship is scuttled (sunk) by its crew a few days later.

December 14 Finland The League of Nations expels the Soviet Union after it fails to halt the war in Finland.

Blitzkrieg

When German troops flooded across the Polish border on the morning of September 1, 1939, they set off a chain of events that set the world at war for six years.

German vehicles stream through the French countryside in May 1940. →

Timeline
1940 January–May

February 16 Norway A British destroyer enters neutral waters off Norway to rescue 299 British merchant sailors held by Germans.

April 9 Norway and Denmark Germans invade, defeating Denmark easily; Norway offers more resistance.

January   February   March   April

March 11 Soviet Union Finland and Soviet Union agree to a peace treaty under which Finland loses 10 percent of its territory; the war has cost 200,000 Soviet dead and 25,000 Finns.

April 14–19 Norway More than 10,000 Allied troops arrive to help Norwegian resistance.

KEY:

Politics

Land war

Sea and air war

In September 1939, Germany attacked an unprepared Poland, which surrendered after heavy losses. Hitler also attacked Norway and Denmark. The British and French were stunned by the speed of the German conquest. For seven months—the so-called Phony War—they prepared for war.

Focus on Norway

On May 10, 1940, Hitler began his western offensive. With aerial support,

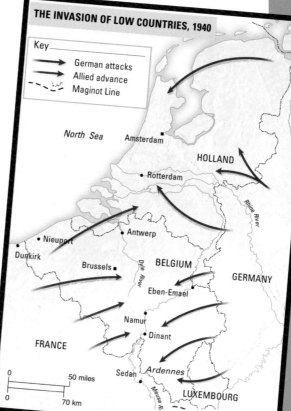

THE INVASION OF LOW COUNTRIES, 1940

Key
→ German attacks
⇒ Allied advance
-·-· Maginot Line

North Sea
Amsterdam
HOLLAND
• Rotterdam
Rhine River
• Nieuport
• Antwerp
Dunkirk
Brussels ■
BELGIUM
Dyle River
Eben-Emael
GERMANY
Namur
• Dinant
FRANCE
Sedan Ardennes
Meuse R.
LUXEMBOURG

0   50 miles
0   70 km

The flat terrain of the Low Countries made the German invasion easier.

Timeline

September 1, 1939 Germans invade Poland.

September 3, 1939 Britain and France declare war.

September 8, 1939 Allied Saar Offensive is soon stopped by Germans.

November 1939 Soviets attack Finland.

April 9, 1940 Germans invade neutral Norway.

May 10, 1940 Germany invades Belgium and Holland.

May 7–10, 1940 British prime minister Neville Chamberlain resigns. Winston Churchill replaces him.

May 12–14, 1940 Germans invade eastern France.

May 26–June 4, 1940 Operation Dynamo rescues British troops from Dunkirk.

June 14, 1940 German troops enter Paris.

June 22, 1940 France surrenders.

← Huge numbers of French refugees flee the German advance on Paris in June 1940.

May 10 Low Countries Nazi paratroopers capture Belgium's key fortress and land in Holland; Allied forces advance into Belgium.

May 12–14 France German forces advance through the Ardennes, driving a wedge between the Allied armies in Belgium and France.

May 28 Belgium King Leopold surrenders as the Allies retreat.

May

May 7–10 Britain Prime Minister Neville Chamberlain resigns and is replaced by Winston Churchill.

May 26 France Operation Dynamo begins to evacuate Allied forces from the port of Dunkirk.

May 31 United States President Franklin D. Roosevelt launches an arms-building program.

Junkers Ju-87

With its screeching siren, the German Junkers Ju-87 dive-bomber—or Stuka, a short version of its full name—spread terror across Europe during the blitzkrieg years. Stuka pilots dove vertically to only 3,000 feet (915 m) above the ground to deliver their bombs accurately. On the battlefield, the Stukas closely supported panzer divisions by attacking enemy forces that might block an advance. They were known as the "flying artillery of the panzers."

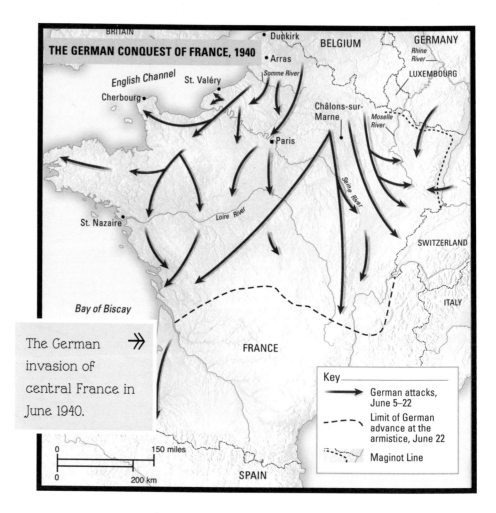

THE GERMAN CONQUEST OF FRANCE, 1940

The German invasion of central France in June 1940.

Key

→ German attacks, June 5–22

--- Limit of German advance at the armistice, June 22

····· Maginot Line

0   150 miles
0   200 km

panzers (tanks) and infantry poured into Belgium and the Netherlands. The Dutch surrendered on May 14.

Trapped in the North

British and French forces fighting in Belgium found themselves outflanked by a German tank advance to the south into France. The government of the new

Timeline
1940
June–
August

June 4 France Operation Dynamo ends; the "little ships" have rescued 338,226 men from the beaches of Dunkirk.

June 10 Italy Italy joins the war on the side of Germany.

June 16–24 France A peace treaty gives Germany control of two-thirds of France; the south is under a puppet French government based at Vichy.

June   July

KEY:

   Politics

Land war

Sea and air war

June 5–10 France Germans launch Operation Red, the advance on Paris. French morale crumbles, and they withdraw south.

June 14 France Germans enter Paris unopposed.

June 30 Channel Islands German troops invade; the islands are the only British home territory occupied during the war.

← Stuka dive-bombers were an essential part of the German tactic of blitzkrieg, or lightning war.

prime minister, Winston Churchill, ordered the British Expeditionary Force to retreat to the port of Dunkirk, from where it was evacuated by the Royal Navy (see box, right). More than 1.2 million Allied soldiers were captured, however. Belgium surrendered on May 28.

The Germans gathered two million troops for an advance on Paris. The city fell without violence on June 14. France surrendered on June 22.

Scandinavia

The Allies pulled out of Norway following the invasion of the Low Countries and France. Germany was now in control of much of northern Europe.

The "Little Ships"

The docks at Dunkirk were full, so the navy called for volunteers to help rescue the army from the beaches. A fleet of "little ships" —commercial or leisure craft—sailed across the English Channel. They rescued some 30,000 men each day in the face of air attack and ferried them to larger vessels offshore. The evacuation ensured the survival of the British army—and perhaps of Britain.

← Allied sailors and troops in a lifeboat after their ship was bombed and sunk off Dunkirk.

July 1 Atlantic Ocean
U-boats begin to inflict heavy losses on Allied convoys; the "Happy Time" lasts until October.

July 21 Eastern Front
Soviets take over Lithuania, Latvia, and Estonia.

August 24–25 Britain The Luftwaffe inflicts serious damage on RAF bases; British air defenses are close to breaking point.

August

July 3 Algeria Fearing French ships will be used by Germans, British attack them and disarm French naval forces in Alexandria, Egypt.

July 10 Britain The Battle of Britain begins when Goering orders attacks on Allied shipping and ports in the English Channel.

August 26–29 Germany The RAF launches night raids on Berlin and other cities; the Germans bomb London in revenge.

Battle of Britain

With the defeat of France and the Low Countries in 1940,
Britain stood alone in Europe against the Nazi threat. It
faced an enemy that was poised to attack its shores.

British pilots rush ⇒
to their planes. The
RAF used radar to
respond swiftly to
any enemy threat.

Timeline
1940
September–
December

KEY:

Politics

Land war

Sea and air war

September

October

September 7 Britain Full-scale
bombing raids on London—the
"Blitz"—begins; the city is
bombed for 57 consecutive days.

September 20–22 Atlantic Ocean
German U-boats launch "wolf pack" operations,
sinking 12 Allied ships; a pack gathers 15 to 20
U-boats for an attack on a convoy.

**September 13–18
Egypt** Italians invade
British-controlled Egypt.

September 27 Germany Germany,
Italy, and Japan agree to the Tripartite
Pact; they will all attack any state that
declares war on any of them.

October 28 Greece
Italian troops invade
Greece from Albania but
meet stiff resistance.

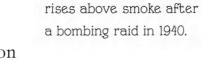
↑ St. Paul's Cathedral rises above smoke after a bombing raid in 1940.

By the summer of 1940, the future looked bleak for the Allies. Hitler ordered the invasion of Britain, code-named Operation Sealion. The invasion faced a major obstacle: the English Channel. In order for German forces to cross it safely, it was vital to defeat the Royal Air Force (RAF).

The Battle of Britain

The two air forces were finely balanced in June 1940, but the RAF did have one advantage. The Chain Home Radar System detected enemy aircraft as they crossed The Channel.

← Spitfires fly in tandem. The British fighters were renowned for their speed and handling.

Timeline

July 10, 1940 The Luftwaffe attacks Allied shipping and ports in The Channel, beginning the Battle of Britain.

July 16, 1940 Hitler plans Operation Sealion, the invasion of Britain, for August 15.

August 24, 1940 German bombs dropped on London.

August 25, 1940 Retaliatory bombing of Berlin.

September 7, 1940 Bombing of London (the "Blitz") begins.

September 15, 1940 Climax of Battle of Britain.

September 17, 1940 Hitler indefinitely postpones Operation Sealion.

May 10–11, 1941 507 German bombers attack London in the largest raid of the Blitz.

November 11–12 Mediterranean Sea At the Battle of Taranto, British aircraft and cruisers devastate the Italian fleet.

December 9–11 Egypt British begin their first offensive in North Africa; some 34,000 Italians are taken prisoner as they retreat rapidly from Egypt.

November   December

November 5 United States President Franklin D. Roosevelt is elected for an unprecedented third term.

November 14 Britain. A nighttime bombing raid on Coventry kills 500 civilians and leaves thousands more homeless.

Winston Churchill (1874–1965)

Born to an aristocratic family, Churchill served as an army officer and war journalist before entering Parliament in 1900. During the 1930s, he was often alone in attacking German expansion. After becoming prime minister in 1939, his words sustained Britain through its "darkest hour." He was key in gaining US support for Britain.

Churchill's famous ➔ "V" sign stood for victory.

British and German airbases during the Battle of Britain. ➔

THE BATTLE OF BRITAIN, 1940

▲ German bomber stations
⚓ German HQ
✦ RAF fighter airfield
⊗ Radar station
○ RAF HQ
···· Limits of fighter command groups
— German fighter limits

From late June until August 12, 1940, RAF and Luftwaffe fighter planes fought dogfights above The Channel. Both sides suffered heavy losses, but British resistance eventually forced Hitler to delay Operation Sealion. The Battle of Britain was a victory for the RAF and its pilots, whom Churchill named "the Few."

The Bombing Campaign

After German bombers accidentally bombed London, Churchill authorized a bombing raid on Berlin. Hitler was enraged. In turn, he ordered the bombing of London and Britain's major cities. However, the need to defend Germany's cities against possible air raids meant that the Luftwaffe had to leave aircraft at home and had fewer to fight the British.

Timeline
1941
January–
April

KEY:

Politics

Land war

Sea and air war

January 2 United States President Roosevelt announces ship-building program to support Allied Atlantic convoys.

February 3 Atlantic Ocean German battle cruisers begin a campaign against Allied merchant ships; they sink 22 vessels before returning to base on March 22.

January

February

February 14 North Africa German general Erwin Rommel's skilled Afrika Korps arrives at Tripoli, Libya, to help the Italians.

The Blitz

Britain was saved from an imminent invasion but the destruction continued. In early September 1940, German bombers began full-scale raids on London and other cities. The capital was bombed for 57 consecutive days. This "Blitz" against civilian and industrial targets continued well into 1944. Its peak was passed by May 1941, however, when Germany pulled aircraft east to invade the Soviet Union. Despite the huge destruction it caused, the Blitz had failed to crush Britain industrially or to destroy the morale of its people.

Air Raids

From September 1940, Londoners got used to almost nightly air raids. Many Londoners slept in cellars, subway stations, or purpose-built air-raid shelters. A "blackout" was put into practice, but German pilots navigated by features such as rivers, so it had little effect. By the end of the Blitz in May 1941, about 40,000 people had died in the raids and huge amounts of property in London and other cities had been destroyed.

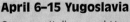
← Onlookers view a bomb crater in front of the Bank of England, London, in January 1941.

March 11 United States President Roosevelt signs the Lend-Lease Act, which allows Britain to get war supplies without paying immediately.

April 6–15 Yugoslavia German, Italian, and Hungarian forces invade Yugoslavia.

March

April

March 28–29 Mediterranean Sea Italian and British fleets clash in the Aegean Sea. Five Italian ships are sunk and 3,000 men are killed for the loss of only one British aircraft.

April 17 Yugoslavia Yugoslavia surrenders but guerrilla forces—partisans— continue a resistance campaign.

April 18–21 Greece British troops sent to help Greeks are forced back to the southern coast by German troops and are evacuated to Crete.

The Battle of the Atlantic

The Battle of the Atlantic began the day Britain declared war on Nazi Germany and ended on May 7, 1945. It was the longest and arguably most important battle of the war.

A British destroyer ➜ escorts merchant ships traveling from the United States to Britain in April 1940.

Timeline
1941
May–
August

May 3–19 Ethiopia The Battle of Amba Alagi in northern Ethiopia ends in Italian surrender to the British.

May 10 Britain Rudolph Hess, deputy leader of the Nazis, flies secretly to Scotland to make a peace deal with the British; he is imprisoned.

May   June

KEY:

 Politics

Land war

Sea and air war

May 10–11 Britain In the largest raid of the Blitz, 507 bombers attack London.

May 20–22 Crete Some 23,000 German troops are attacked by British, New Zealand, and Australian troops, but they gain a foothold.

May 28–31 Crete The Germans take Crete. Losses are similar on both German and British sides.

The German battleship *Bismarck* fires at HMS *Hood* in the Battle of ⬇ Denmark Strait.

Timeline

September 3, 1939 German U-30 sinks British passenger liner *Athenia*. First act of long campaign.

December 13, 1939 Battle of River Plate in neutral Uruguay.

May 1941 Battle of Denmark Strait results in the destruction of the most powerful German battleship, *Bismarck*.

August 1941 Start of the Arctic War.

December 11, 1941 United States enters the war.

July 1942 United States adopts convoy system after heavy naval losses.

December 1942 HMS *Audacity*, a new generation of small escort carriers, is sunk.

November 12, 1944 Pride of the German navy, the *Tirpitz*, finally destroyed.

May 1945 German navy surrenders.

⬅ German U-boat technicians prepare torpedoes in 1941.

At the start of the war, Britain's Royal Navy was the largest in the world. The much smaller German navy, the Kriegsmarine, could not hope to take on the British fleet. Instead, the Germans planned to sink merchant vessels carrying supplies to Britain, mainly from North America. The Germans' key weapon was the U-boat (short for Unterseeboot, the German word for submarine). Hunting in "wolf packs," the U-boats preyed on undefended vessels. The task was so easy the U-boat crews called the early part of the war the "Happy Time."

June 15–17 North Africa The British launch Operation Battle-axe to relieve troops trapped by the Afrika Korps in the Libyan port of Tobruk, but they stop after heavy tank losses.

July 4 Yugoslavia Joseph Broz, known as "Tito," emerges as leader of Yugoslav partisans.

July

August

June 22 Soviet Union Germany launches Operation Barbarossa to invade the Soviet Union with three million men; German air attacks quickly destroy 1,800 Soviet aircraft on the ground.

July 16 Soviet Union Around 300,000 Red Army troops and 3,200 tanks are trapped near Smolensk.

July 31 Germany Reinhard Heydrich, head of the SS secret police, ordered to plan extermination of Europe's Jews: the "Final Solution."

U-boat Tactics

Initially U-boats hunted alone, usually attacking targets in daylight when submerged. As more U-boats were built, they hunted in "wolf packs" of 15 to 20 vessels that attacked together at night. The tactic began in fall 1940 and was successful until 1943. Britain's initial lack of escort vessels meant that there was little risk to the U-boats. Later, faster escorts, sonar equipment, and increased air power doomed the wolf packs to defeat.

The Convoy System

Britain adopted a convoy system in which groups of merchant ships could be escorted by warships. However, Britain lacked convoy escort ships, and its vessels were ineffective at hunting U-boats. By the end of 1940, Britain seemed close to losing the Battle of the Atlantic. By December 1940, the British had lost 20 percent of their merchant fleet. In contrast, the Germans had lost just six U-boats.

Britain Fights Back

The Allies slowly discovered better ways to defeat the German threat. Long-range aircraft provided air cover, while mines and other innovations made it easier to destroy U-boats. In May 1941, Germany's most powerful battleship, *Bismarck*, was damaged in the Battle of Denmark Strait and was then hunted down and destroyed. It was a huge boost to British morale.

U-boats spent long periods on the surface, but went underwater when they attacked in daylight. ⇓

Timeline
1941
September–
December

September 3 **Poland** Successful experiments to kill Jewish prisoners in gas chambers are carried out in Auschwitz camp.

September 19 **Soviet Union** The Germans take Kiev.

September

October

KEY:

 Politics

Land war

Sea and air war

September 4 **Atlantic Ocean** A U-boat mistakes the US destroyer *Greer* for a British vessel and attacks it; US warships are ordered to "shoot on sight" any U-boats they see.

September 30 **Soviet Union** The Germans begin Operation Typhoon, the attack on Moscow.

↑ Survivors from a sinking ship row to a U-boat to be taken prisoner.

Help from the United States

After the United States entered the war in December 1941, it suffered heavy losses of merchant shipping as U-boats patrolled the East Coast. The Germans referred to early 1942 as a second "Happy Time." It was shortlived, however. As Allied antisubmarine tactics and technology improved, they were able to destroy the U-boats in large numbers. As German losses mounted, the U-boats were withdrawn to France, where they were kept in port. After the Allied invasion of France in June 1944, many of the submarines were destroyed. The Germans had effectively lost the Battle of the Atlantic.

The Enigma Code

Enigma was used by the Germans to transmit complex codes that changed daily. British intelligence even built one of the first-ever computers, Colossus, to help crack the code. A breakthrough came in March 1941, when an Enigma machine was found on a captured U-boat. It allowed the British to decipher information that proved vital to the Allied victory.

← Enigma had a system of rotors that turned messages into code.

December 7 Hawaii Japanese aircraft attack the US fleet at Pearl Harbor, killing 2,000 people and destroying six battleships.

December 8 Soviet Union Adolf Hitler halts the advance on Moscow for the winter; the German panzers cannot operate in the freezing temperatures.

November

December

November 18–26 North Africa British relieve Tobruk despite heavy losses; Rommel retreats.

December 11 United States Germany and Italy declare war on the United States, which declares war on them in return.

December 18–19 Egypt Italian midget submarines, each with only two operators, sink two British battleships in Alexandria, Egypt.

Operation Barbarossa

Operation Barbarossa was the most ambitious campaign of World War II. Hitler invaded the Soviet Union to gain lebensraum ("living space") for the German people.

German Mark III panzers advance on the Eastern Front. ⇉

Timeline
1942 January– April

January 5 Soviet Union Stalin's troops counterattack; their initial success halts as the Germans set up well-defended areas known as "hedgehogs."

January 16–19 Germany Hitler sacks more than 30 of his senior generals because they want to withdraw in the face of Soviet attacks on the Eastern Front.

January

February

KEY:

Europe and North Africa

Pacific

Sea and air war

January 13 Atlantic Ocean U-boats attack shipping off the East Coast of the United States.

January 20 Germany The "Final Solution"—the extermination of Europe's Jews—becomes key to Nazi war plans at the Wannsee Conference in Berlin.

THE INVASION OF THE SOVIET UNION, JUNE 1941

Key
→ German attacks
— German front line, June 22, 1941
- - - German front line, August 25, 1941
▨ Trapped Soviet units

SWEDEN
Helsinki
Leningrad
Stockholm
ESTONIA
Moscow
LATVIA Riga
LITHUANIA
Copenhagen
Baltic Sea
Smolensk
Army Group North
Bryansk
EAST PRUSSIA
Minsk
GERMANY
Kursk
Berlin
Warsaw
Brest
Pripet Marshes
SOVIET UNION
Army Group Center
POLAND
Kiev
Kharkov
Prague
Bohemia
Dnieper River
Stalingrad
SLOVAKIA
UKRAINE
Danube River
Vienna
AUSTRIA
HUNGARY
Army Group South
YUGOSLAVIA
ROMANIA
Bucharest

0   300 miles
0   500 km

↑ German progress was fast along the 1,000-mile (1,600 km) Soviet front.

The German High Command began planning Operation Barbarossa in summer 1940, despite the nonaggression pact signed with the Soviets in 1939. Hitler claimed that Stalin was preparing to attack Germany. Stalin did indeed have many troops on his western borders, but they were mainly defensive.

Forces and Tactics

The Germans gathered one of the largest invasion forces ever assembled. The offensive had three massive thrusts:

Timeline

Summer 1940 German High Command plans Operation Barbarossa.

Spring 1941 Soviet divisions mass along western border.

June 22, 1941 German artillery opens fire on Soviet troops.

Late June, 1941 Minsk captured.

Mid July, 1941 Smolensk captured.

July 3, 1941 Stalin launches his "scorched earth" policy; troops destroy anything that could fall into German hands.

August 21, 1941 Hitler orders forces to concentrate on advance through Ukraine.

September 19, 1941 Kiev falls to the Germans.

← German artillery opens fire on the Eastern Front in the early hours of June 22, 1941.

February 11–12 North Sea The Channel Dash sees German battle cruisers speed to the North Sea before the British can stop them.

February 27–29 Java Sea The Japanese inflict heavy losses on an Allied fleet.

April 9 Philippines US and Filipino forces in the Philippines surrender to the Japanese. Many die on a 65-mile (105 km) forced march into captivity.

March   April

February 14 Singapore The British at Singapore surrender to the Japanese.

March 28–29 France British commandos attack the St. Nazaire dry dock, used by the Germans to repair warships, but 144 men are killed in the raid and many more are captured.

April 18 Japan In a raid led by James Doolittle, 16 US B-25 bombers launched from an aircraft carrier attack Tokyo; Japan's leaders decide to seek a battle to destroy US naval power in the Pacific.

Soviet Factories Move East

Factories in the western Soviet Union were threatened by the German advance in fall of 1941. So entire factories were dismantled, put onto railroad cars, and moved east to the safety of the Ural Mountains. Up to 25 million workers also moved. They went straight back to work in the new factories. Even in freezing winter temperatures, production never stopped.

toward Leningrad (now called St. Petersburg); toward Kiev, the capital of Ukraine; and toward Smolensk, west of Moscow.

Despite the warning signs, Stalin and his generals were taken by surprise when German artillery opened fire along the Soviet border at 3:30 A.M. on June 22, 1941. The invasion had begun.

A T-34 rolls off the production line in a factory in a city named "Tankograd." ⬇

The Advance Slows

In the first weeks, the German invasion seemed unstoppable. German panzers advanced far into the Soviet Union. By mid-July, however, the advance had slowed down. Muddy roads delayed German supplies, and the advancing troops could not rely on finding food or fuel. Stalin had ordered a "scorched earth" policy, which meant that crops, fuel, and any other potentially useful resources were destroyed by the retreating Soviets. The

Timeline
1942 May– August

May 26–31 North Africa The Battle of Gazala. Rommel attacks the British, but his tanks suffer serious fuel problems until the Italians provide supplies on May 31.

June 4 Pacific Ocean US naval forces win a decisive victory over the Japanese at the Battle of Midway.

May

June

May 31 Germany Britain launches its first "1,000 bomber raid" on Cologne; 59,000 people are left homeless.

June 10–13 North Africa Rommel's way to Tobruk is open as British withdraw after the Battle of Gazala.

June 21 North Africa Rommel captures Tobruk.

KEY:

 Europe and North Africa

Pacific

 Sea and air war

The German advances made significant gains in the first six months of the invasion. →

OPERATION BARBAROSSA, JUNE–DECEMBER 1941

Key
→ German attacks
— German front line, June 26, 1941
--- German front line, December 5, 1941
▨ Trapped Soviet troops

tenacity of the Red Army's defense also surprised German commanders.

The Fall of Kiev

Over the opposition of his High Command, Hitler ordered his troops to advance to Kiev. On September 15, two panzer groups encircled the city. It fell on September 19, 1941, despite Stalin's order that it should be defended at all costs.

Hitler hailed the encirclement of Kiev as "the greatest battle in world history." Many of his commanders, however, saw it as a strategic error that distracted them from their primary target: the advance on Moscow.

The Siege of Leningrad

As German troops closed in on Leningrad in fall 1941, some 700,000 of its three million inhabitants fled. Rationing began for the remainder, but people began to die of starvation as supply routes were cut off. In January 1942, however, Lake Ladoga froze and it became possible to drive trucks across it. The Soviets built a road 20 miles (32 km) long across the ice, which became known as the "Road of Life." The siege was broken in January 1944 after the Germans were forced to retreat.

June 28 Soviet Union The Germans launch summer offensive, Operation Blue, into southern Russia to capture oil fields in the Caucasus.

August 7 Guadalcanal US Marines land on Guadalcanal and face fierce Japanese resistance.

July

August

July 4–10 Soviet Union After a two-month siege, the Germans capture the port of Sevastopol and about 90,000 Red Army troops.

August 19 France A combined Canadian, British, and American force attacks the port of Dieppe. It is a disaster, with most men killed.

August 23 Soviet Union A raid by 600 German bombers on Stalingrad kills thousands.

North Africa

The war in the North African deserts saw Axis and Allied
troops fight for two years to control the region and gain
access to the oil fields of the Middle East.

British troops defend →
the Gazala Line. They
fire a 25-pounder gun,
one of the best field
guns of the war.

Timeline
1942
September –
December

September 2 Poland The Nazis
"clear" the Jewish Warsaw Ghetto;
more than 50,000 Jews are killed.

September

October

KEY:

Europe and
North Africa

Pacific

Sea and
air war

October 23 North Africa
The Second Battle of El
Alamein begins in Egypt.

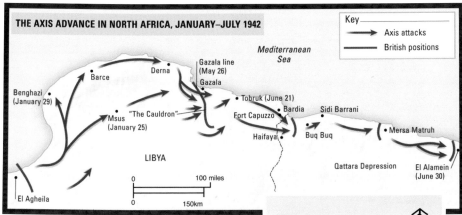

THE AXIS ADVANCE IN NORTH AFRICA, JANUARY–JULY 1942

Key
→ Axis attacks
— British positions

Mediterranean Sea

Gazala line (May 26)
Gazala
Barce
Derna
Benghazi (January 29)
"The Cauldron"
Msus (January 25)
Tobruk (June 21)
Fort Capuzzo · Bardia
Sidi Barrani
Haifaya · Buq Buq
Mersa Matruh
LIBYA
Qattara Depression
El Alamein (June 30)
El Agheila

0   100 miles
0   150km

Axis troops made significant advances in Africa between January and July 1942. ⇑

Fighting in Africa began in 1940. Italian dictator Benito Mussolini hoped to create an empire there. British troops fought back the Italians, but the advantage swung back to the Axis with the arrival of the German Afrika Korps under General Erwin Rommel in early 1941.

Rommel broke through the Allied lines at Gazala, captured the port of Tobruk, and

Timeline

January 1942 Germans prepare for new offensive.
July 1, 1942 1st Battle of El Alamein starts as Rommel attacks Allied troops.
July 22, 1942 Rommel calls off offensive.
August 1942 Churchill makes Montgomery commander of the 8th Army.
August 30, 1942 Battle of Alam Halfa.
October 23, 1942 2nd Battle of El Alamein.
November 8, 1942 Operation Torch begins.
February 19–25, 1943 Battle of Kasserine Pass. US troops defeated.
March 26, 1943 Allied troops break through behind Mareth Line.
May 13, 1943 Axis forces surrender in North Africa.

⇐ The First Battle of El Alamein halted Rommel's advance, but with 13,000 casualties.

November 19 Soviet Union General Georgi Zhukov launches an attack to relieve Stalingrad; the pincer movement traps the Germans fighting in the city and the German front collapses.

November   December

November 2–24 North Africa The Second Battle of El Alamein. Rommel is forced to retreat; it is the first major defeat suffered by German forces during the war.

December 19 Soviet Union A German counterattack fails to rescue the Sixth Army trapped in Stalingrad, where conditions are deteriorating and food is short.

Malta's Resistance

The Mediterranean island of Malta, a British possession, was a base for attacks on Axis supply lines to North Africa. In 1941, Hitler ordered the Luftwaffe to bomb the island into surrender. Against all odds, the island held out against remarkable pressure. That enabled Allied attacks on Axis shipping to continue until 1943.

⬅ Captured German soldiers in the desert wait to be taken to a prisoner-of-war camp.

headed east toward Egypt. The Allies retreated to a defensive line at the village of El Alamein. There, on October 23, 1942, some 195,000 Allied troops under Field Marshal Bernard Montgomery clashed with 105,000 Axis soldiers.

Battles of El Alamein

Fighting continued through November until, after some three weeks, Rommel gave up. He retreated more than

Operation Torch was the first US campaign of the war in the west. ⟩⟩

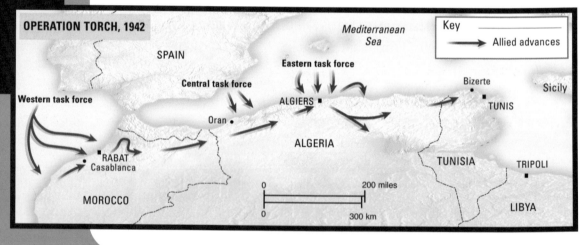

OPERATION TORCH, 1942

SPAIN
Western task force
Central task force
Eastern task force
Mediterranean Sea
Key
→ Allied advances
RABAT
Casablanca
Oran
ALGIERS
ALGERIA
Bizerte
TUNIS
Sicily
TUNISIA
TRIPOLI
MOROCCO
LIBYA
0   200 miles
0   300 km

Timeline
1943
January – April

January 31 Guadalcanal US troops finally capture the island of Guadalcanal in the Pacific after six months' fighting.

February 2 Soviet Union The Siege of Stalingrad ends when 93,000 German troops surrender.

February 18 Burma British Chindits parachute behind Japanese lines for a six-week mission to raid enemy supply lines.

January   February

January 18 Poland Jewish fighters in the Warsaw Ghetto begin attacking German troops.

February 14–22 North Africa Inexperienced US troops suffer heavy losses in the Battle of Kasserine Pass.

February 16 Germany Students demonstrate against Hitler's regime in Munich; the leaders are executed.

KEY:
- Europe and North Africa
- Pacific
- Sea and air war

↑ US troops bring a gun ashore in the joint US-British invasion of northwest Africa.

1,000 miles (1,600 km) back into Tunisia. El Alamein was the first major defeat suffered by the Germans during the war.

Operation Torch

At the same time, the United States joined the war in North Africa. US troops landed in Morocco to join Operation Torch to rid the region of Axis forces. After heavy fighting, the Allies threatened to encircle the Germans, who retreated. Rommel returned to Germany, and after a final Allied push, Axis forces in North Africa surrendered.

Afrika Korps

Rommel's Afrika Korps staged a daring offensive in early 1942 with a small but well-equipped force that pushed the British back into Egypt. But by summer 1942, the Korps needed supplies and was undermanned. Hitler refused requests for more resources. At El Alamein, Panzer Group Afrika was forced into a long retreat by the better-supplied British Eighth Army. Rommel was recalled from Africa on March 6, 1943. The decimated Axis forces in North Africa surrendered on May 13.

March 14 Soviet Union German forces destroy the Soviet Third Tank Army, forcing Soviets to abandon newly won territory on the Eastern Front.

April 12 Soviet Union The Germans find a mass grave in Katyn Forest containing the bodies of 10,000 Polish army officers executed by the Soviet secret police in 1939.

March

April

March 15 Soviet Union The Germans launch Operation Citadel, a plan to destroy Red Army troops near the city of Kursk.

April 17 Germany US bombers attack the German city of Bremen.

Sicily and Italy

In 1943, the Allies began a campaign to invade Europe from the south by targeting Sicily. They hoped that occupying the island would knock Italy out of the war.

An American soldier → leads a convoy of German prisoners in Sicily, 1944.

Timeline
1943
May–August

May 13 North Africa Axis forces surrender to the Allies; 620,000 Axis casualties and prisoners have been lost in the campaign.

May 16–17 Germany The Dambusters Raid. The British use "bouncing bombs" to destroy dams in Germany's industrial Ruhr region.

May　　　　　June　　　　　July

May 16 Poland The Warsaw Ghetto uprising ends; it has been harshly repressed by the Germans.

June 10 Germany British and US bombers begin Operation Pointblank, a year-long series of attacks on German industry.

July 5 Soviet Union The Battle of Kursk is the largest tank battle in history; the Germans make little progress against the Soviets.

KEY:

 Europe and North Africa

Pacific

 Sea and air war

After the conquest of North Africa, the Allies planned an attack on Sicily to provide a base for a move to the Italian mainland. It would also divert as many Germans as possible from northwest Europe.

The invasion of Sicily, code-named Operation Husky, was an amphibious (land and sea) assault. For almost a month, Allied aircraft dropped thousands of tons of bombs on airfields, ports, bridges, rail links, and supply depots. British and US paratroopers and

ALLIED INVASION OF SICILY, 1943

Key
→ Allied attacks
--- Front line, July 18
— Front line, August 3

0   50 miles
0   80 km

← Allied troops landed on the south side of Sicily.

Timeline

January 1943 Allied leaders decide to capture Sicily before invading Italy.

April/May 1943 Operation Mincemeat fools Hitler into diverting defenders to Greece and Sardinia.

July 10, 1943 Operation Husky begins.

July 25, 1943 Mussolini fired.

September 3, 1943 Italians sign armistice with the Allies.

September 9, 1943 Allied troops land in southern Italy.

September 16, 1943 German troops withdraw north.

May 11–18, 1944 Allies break through the Gustav Line at Monte Cassino.

June 5, 1944 US troops enter Rome.

April 29, 1945 German forces in northern Italy surrender.

British troops wade ashore during the Allied invasion of Sicily, 1943. →

July 12–13 Soviet Union The Soviets narrowly defeat the Germans at Kursk. The battle leaves 500,000 casualties dead, injured, or missing.

July 25 Italy The king of Italy sacks Benito Mussolini. The new leader, Pietro Badoglio, hopes that the Allies will occupy Italy before it falls under German control.

August

July 10 Sicily Operation Husky. US and British troops invade the island.

July 24–August 2 Germany The British bomb Hamburg, killing around 50,000 civilians and leaving 800,000 homeless.

August 17 Sicily The capture of Messina marks Allied victory on Sicily; from there, the Allies can attack the Italian peninsula.

Rescue of Mussolini

Hitler sent the SS officer Otto Skorzeny to rescue Mussolini from imprisonment in a hotel high in the central Italian mountains. Using gliders, Skorzeny's assault force mounted a daring rescue and flew Mussolini to Vienna. He became head of a puppet German state in northern Italy, known as the Republic of Salo.

Mussolini (right) is escorted to a waiting aircraft after his rescue. ⇒

⤒ The Italians sign the armistice with the Allies on September 3, 1943.

glider-borne troops landed on July 9, 1943. The island's Italian defenders soon gave up, but German resistance was far stronger. Eventually, the Allied numerical superiority won. The Germans retreated across the Strait of Messina to the mainland.

Italy Surrenders

Italy's politicians now sought a way out of the war. King Victor Emmanuel III sacked Mussolini on July 25, 1943. The former dictator was arrested and imprisoned in a remote hotel in the Apennine mountains. The Italians surrendered on September 3. Furious at the loss of his ally, Hitler sent troops to occupy northern Italy while the Germans retreating from Sicily seized the capital, Rome, and dug in at a defensive line to the south.

The Allies landed from Sicily at Salerno on September 9. They created a bridgehead and

Timeline
1943 September–December

September 9 Italy US and British troops land in southern Italy.

September 12 Italy German airborne troops led by Lieutenant Colonel Otto Skorzeny rescue Mussolini from imprisonment in a hotel high in the Italian mountains.

September

October

September 25 Soviet Union The Red Army recaptures Smolensk.

October 12–22 Italy Allied forces advance slowly north in bad weather toward German positions on the Gustav Line, in central Italy.

KEY:
- Europe and North Africa
- Pacific
- Sea and air war

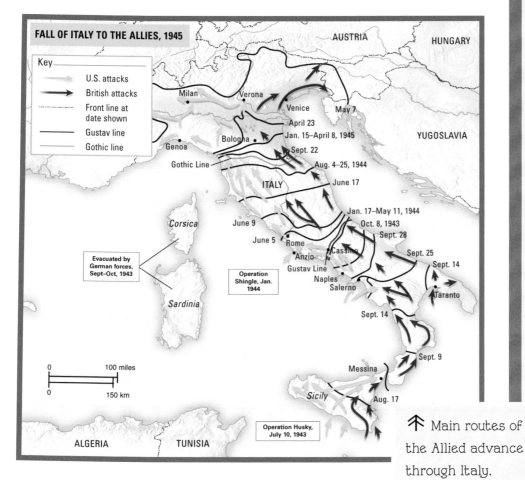

FALL OF ITALY TO THE ALLIES, 1945

Key
- U.S. attacks
- British attacks
- Front line at date shown
- Gustav line
- Gothic line

AUSTRIA   HUNGARY

Milan   Verona   Venice   May 7
April 23
Jan. 15–April 8, 1945   YUGOSLAVIA
Bologna   Sept. 22
Genoa   Aug. 4–25, 1944
Gothic Line   June 17

ITALY

Corsica   Jan. 17–May 11, 1944
June 9   Oct. 8, 1943
June 5   Rome   Sept. 28

Evacuated by German forces, Sept–Oct, 1943   Anzio   Cassino   Sept. 25
Gustav Line   Sept. 14

Operation Shingle, Jan. 1944   Naples   Salerno
Sardinia   Taranto

Sept. 14

Sept. 9
0   100 miles
0   150 km   Messina
Sicily   Aug. 17

ALGERIA   TUNISIA   Operation Husky, July 10, 1943

↑ Main routes of the Allied advance through Italy.

The Fall of Italy

With the invasion of Sicily, Italian politicians feared Italy might be next. To avoid destruction, they signed an armistice with the Allies on September 3. In response, German troops seized key targets across Italy. As the Germans completed their invasion, Allied troops arrived in the south. Fierce fighting followed. Although the Allies gained the upper hand, no immediate victory was forthcoming. Italy, however, was no longer a free agent: it was an occupied country.

began to fight their way north. German resistance was strong, however. It would not be until May 1944 that the Allies broke through the defensive line at Monte Cassino. That breakthrough also liberated US troops who had become trapped after landing behind German lines at Anzio. On June 5, 1944, US troops entered Rome. Fighting in the north continued until April 1945, when the Germans surrendered.

November 20 Gilbert Islands US Marines land on Tawara and Bieto in the Gilbert Islands in the Pacific Ocean.

November 28 Iran British prime minister Winston Churchill, President Roosevelt, and Soviet leader Joseph Stalin meet in Tehran; they give priority to a cross-channel invasion of occupied Europe in May 1944.

November   December

November 6 Soviet Union The Red Army captures Kiev, trapping the German Seventeenth Army in the Crimea.

December 26 Arctic Ocean The Battle of the North Cape sees British warships sink German battleship *Scharnhorst*.

Stalingrad

By late spring 1942, the Germans had recovered from near disaster outside Moscow during the freezing winter and had renewed their efforts to defeat Stalin.

During fighting, German infantry take cover in a Stalingrad trench. →

Timeline
1944
January–
April

January 14–17 Soviet Union. Red Army attacks on the Germans besieging Leningrad force the Germans to retreat. Some 830,000 civilians have died in the three-year siege.

January 22 Italy Allied troops land at Anzio, behind the Gustav Line, and meet little resistance; but US general John Lucas orders his forces to dig in and create defensive positions.

January

February

KEY:

Europe

Pacific

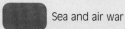
Sea and air war

January 30 Marshall Islands Americans begin an attack on the Marshall Islands in the Pacific.

February 4–24 Burma The Japanese launch operation Ha-Go to drive the Allies back to the border with India.

With Leningrad under siege in the north, in June 1942 the Germans launched Operation Blue into southern Russia. Initially the German troops streamed across the vast Russian steppes. They met little resistance. Stalin had been persuaded to surrender territory in order to gain time. Soviet forces withdrew as German forces advanced toward Stalingrad. The industrial city on the Volga River was strategically vital to halting the German advance.

Soviet general Georgi ⍓ Zhukov led the defense of Stalingrad.

Timeline

January 5, 1942 Stalin orders counterattack against German invaders.

June 28, 1942 Germans launch Operation Blue, summer offensive into southern Russia.

July 4–10, 1942 2-month siege ends with German capture of port of Sevastopol.

August 23, 1942 Raid by 600 German bombers on Stalingrad kills thousands.

November 19, 1942 Soviets launch attack to free Stalingrad. The rapid pincer movement traps Germans in the city and their front collapses.

December 19, 1942 Germans fail to rescue Sixth Army trapped in Stalingrad.

February 2, 1943 Siege ends when 93,000 German troops surrender.

Under Attack

In August 1942, the Luftwaffe began bombing Stalingrad, reducing much of the city to rubble. As German troops entered the city, however, they met stubborn resistance. Fighting raged through the ruins. Soviet civilians

⟵ Soviet infantry fight in the ruins of Stalingrad.

March 20–22 Italy Allied attacks fail to overcome Monte Cassino, part of the Gustav Line.

March

April

February 18–22 Marshall Islands US forces seize Eniwetok Atoll, completing the conquest of the islands.

Snipers at War

Stalingrad's ruins were ideal for snipers. Red Army sharpshooters picked off their victims from hidden positions. They lay immobile for hours and used their telescopic sights to find a target. Male and female Russian snipers killed hundreds of German officers and spread great fear. They were rewarded with improved food and quarters.

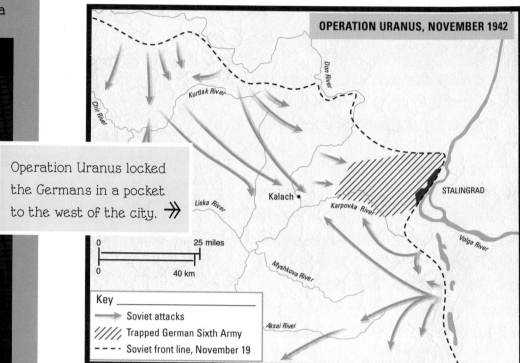

OPERATION URANUS, NOVEMBER 1942

Operation Uranus locked the Germans in a pocket to the west of the city. ⟫

Don River

Kurtlak River

Chir River

Liska River

Kalach

Karpovka River

STALINGRAD

Volga River

Myshkova River

Aksai River

0   25 miles
0   40 km

Key
→ Soviet attacks
/// Trapped German Sixth Army
- - - Soviet front line, November 19

lived in cellars and sewers, surviving on food they found in the pockets of the dead. The Germans could not, however, dislodge Soviet troops from the small areas of the city they still held, despite almost continual bombardment. German attacks grew less frequent and were all but over by November 12.

The Soviet sniper Vasily Zaitsev (on the left) killed more than 200 Germans. ⟫

Defeat of the Sixth Army

The Soviets began a counterattack. On November 19, General Georgi Zhukov launched a rapid pincer

Timeline
1944 May– August

May 11–18 Italy The Allies break through the Gustav Line near Monte Cassino.

June 6 Northern France D-Day. The Allied invasion of Normandy, Operation Overlord, begins with paratroopers landing to seize key targets and amphibious landings on five beaches. By the end of the day, the Allies have a beachhead in Europe at the cost of 2,500 dead.

May   June

KEY:

 Europe

 Pacific

■ Sea and air war

May 9 Soviet Union The Red Army liberates the Black Sea port of Sevastopol.

June 3 Italy German troops abandon Rome, which is occupied by US troops on June 5.

June 19–21 Philippine Sea The "Great Marianas Turkey Shoot." The Japanese lose three aircraft carriers and 460 combat aircraft in the Battle of the Philippine Sea.

↑ Soviet infantry advance through the ruins of Stalingrad.

movement that trapped the Germans in the city. They suffered from bitterly cold weather and a shortage of food. Meanwhile, Hitler called off plans to rescue the Sixth Army. The troops were on their own.

Surrender in the Snow

The German commander Friedrich Paulus asked Hitler to be allowed to open negotiations with the Soviets. Hitler refused and made it clear that he wanted Paulus to commit suicide. Instead, Paulus surrendered his 93,000 men on February 2, 1943. The Soviet Union had won a great victory.

Disobeying Hitler

On January 30, 1943, Hilter promoted the commander of the Sixth Army, Friedrich Paulus, to field marshal. Rather than a reward, however, the promotion was a signal that Paulus should commit suicide rather than surrender. No German officer of such a rank had ever surrendered. Paulus ignored Hitler; he surrendered and spent the rest of the war as a prisoner.

← Friedrich Paulus was released by the Soviets in 1953. While in captivity, he had become a critic of the Nazi leadership.

June 30 Britain To date, 2,000 V1 "flying bombs" have been launched against British targets, mostly London.

July 20 Germany German officers try to kill Hitler. Count Schenk von Stauffenberg plants a bomb in a conference room, but fails to kill Hitler. The failure leads to the execution of dozens of suspects.

July

August

June 22 Soviet Union With huge numerical superiority, the Red Army launches Operation Bagration against German Army Group Center.

August 1 Poland The Warsaw Uprising: 38,000 soldiers of the Polish Home Army fight the Germans.

August 25 France General Dietrich von Choltitz, commander of the German garrison in Paris, surrenders the city to the Allies.

D-Day: Operation Overlord

The D-Day landings remain the greatest amphibious
assault of all time. The landings hastened Nazi Germany's
defeat, but were a major gamble by the western Allies.

US infantry land on
Omaha Beach late on
June 6, 1944. ⇒

Timeline
1944
September–
December

September 2 Finland Finland accepts
a peace treaty with the Soviet Union
and severs relations with Germany.

October 2 Poland After a
two-month battle, the last Poles
in Warsaw surrender to the
Germans; 150,000 Poles have died.

September   October

KEY:

Europe

Pacific

Sea and air war

September 17 Holland
Operation Market Garden. The Allies
suffer heavy losses as paratroopers
try to seize key bridges.

September 22–25 Holland
Paratroopers retreat from
Arnhem.

In early June 1944, southern Britain became a vast armed camp as Allied forces prepared for the most complex military operation ever attempted: landing huge numbers of troops across The Channel.

The Allies had selected Normandy in northern France as the site for the landings. They sent fake signals by radio in order to divert the Germans into believing that the invasion would come farther to the northeast.

↑ Loaded landing craft speed toward the Normandy coast.

Timeline

January 1943 Countdown to D-Day begins.

May 29, 1944 Allied troops begin moving to ports along the south coast of England.

June 3, 1944 All ready, waiting for weather to turn favorable.

June 5, 1944 7,000 warships leave for Normandy.

June 6, 1944 D-Day. Allied invasion of Normandy, Operation Overlord, begins.

June 10, 1944 German soldiers kill 642 civilians in Oradour-sur-Glane as retaliation for attacks on panzer division by French Resistance.

June 13, 1944 27 British tanks are destroyed in battle in Villers-Bocage, Normandy.

August 25, 1944 German garrison commander in Paris surrenders to Allies.

← The five invasion beaches were captured on D-Day, but the Allies did not move inland.

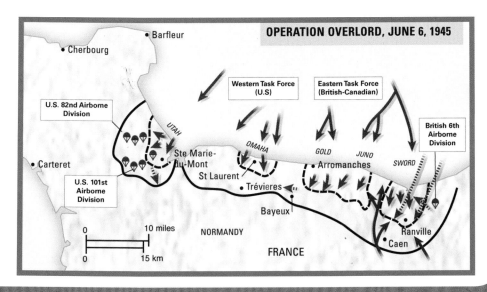

OPERATION OVERLORD, JUNE 6, 1945

- Barfleur
- Cherbourg
- U.S. 82nd Airborne Division
- UTAH
- Western Task Force (U.S)
- Eastern Task Force (British-Canadian)
- British 6th Airborne Division
- OMAHA
- GOLD
- JUNO
- SWORD
- Ste Marie-du-Mont
- St Laurent
- Arromanches
- Carteret
- U.S. 101st Airborne Division
- Trévieres
- Bayeux
- Ranville
- Caen
- NORMANDY
- FRANCE

0   10 miles
0   15 km

October 20 Philippines The US Sixth Army lands on Leyte Island in the Philippines; US general Douglas MacArthur keeps a promise he made two years earlier: "I shall return."

December 16 Belgium Hitler begins Operation Watch on the Rhine, which aims to capture Antwerp. The Germans advance in thick fog. They are stopped by US paratroopers in Bastogne.

November

December

October 23–26 Philippines
The Japanese Combined Fleet is defeated heavily at the Battle of Leyte Gulf.

Dwight D. Eisenhower

People doubted the Allied Supreme Commander had enough experience to lead the invasion. Eisenhower proved them wrong, partly thanks to his combat experience in North Africa. His strategy of advancing on a broad front in northwest Europe in late 1944 is widely judged to have been correct.

The Allied High Command for D-Day included Eisenhower (front, center) and Field Marshal Bernard Montgomery (front, right).➤➤

On June 3, bad weather delayed Operation Overlord. On June 5, an improvement in the weather for about 24 hours allowed some 7,000 warships and landing craft to set out for Normandy.

D-Day

Shortly after midnight on June 6, US and British paratroopers successfully landed inland from the five landing beaches to capture vital roads and bridges. The landings themselves took place after an artillery bombardment from Allied warships and an attack from Allied bombers on German positions.

The Landings

The landings met different degrees of resistance. US troops landed on Utah Beach at 6:31 A.M.,

↑ US troops help a colleague on Omaha Beach.

Timeline
1945 January–March

January 28 Belgium The German Ardennes offensive has cost about 100,000 German lives, with about 81,000 US casualties.

January 30 Germany Soviet forces reach the Oder River, only 100 miles (160 km) from Berlin.

February 4 Soviet Union Stalin, Roosevelt, and Churchill meet at Yalta to decide the division of postwar Europe.

January

February

KEY:

Europe

Pacific

Sea and air war

January 27 Poland The Red Army liberates the Nazi death camp at Auschwitz.

February 3 Philippines US forces enter Manila, capital of the Philippines; Japanese forces virtually destroy the city.

just a minute behind schedule. By nightfall on D-Day, some 23,000 men and 1,700 vehicles had gone ashore with few casualties. Only 10 miles (16 km) to the east, however, Omaha Beach was nearly a disaster. Due to Allied mistakes, some 2,300 US troops were killed.

Anglo-Canadian Landings

On Gold, Sword, and Juno beaches, which stretched for 25 miles (40 km), British and Canadian forces met relatively little resistance. By late morning, all three invasion groups were also pushing inland. They were helped because the Germans had their panzer divisions farther to the northeast.

Members of the maquis and Free French troops during the invasion of Normandy.

Despite the massive success of D-Day, however, the Allies had failed in one goal. They had not pushed inland as far as they had hoped. This had repercussions in the following weeks as the Germans fought back with great determination. The Allies still faced weeks of bloody combat in order to break out of Normandy and advance first into France and then across the Rhine River into Germany itself.

The Resistance

The Allied invasion was supported by the French Resistance. British and US agents went to Normandy before D-Day to deliver weapons and get intelligence. They helped organize sabotage attacks on railroads that the Germans might use to get reinforcements to the coast. Railroad workers also staged go-slows. The Germans believed it was this action, not the Resistance or Allied bombings, that made France's rail system unworkable.

February 14 Germany As the Red Army advance, half of the 2.3 million population of German East Prussia flees west. Thousands die from cold or exhaustion.

March 7 Japan A US bombing raid on Tokyo kills 100,000 people and destroys a large area of the Japanese capital.

March

February 13–14 Germany British bombers bomb Dresden, creating a firestorm that kills at least 50,000 people.

February 17 Iwo Jima US Marines land on the island of Iwo Jima, which they capture after a month of heavy fighting.

March 23 Germany British and US forces start to cross the Rhine River. German troops offer little resistance.

The Fall of Germany

At the start of 1945, the Third Reich was being crushed between forces from both east and west. Armageddon was about to descend upon the people of Germany.

A Soviet soldier raises the Red Flag of the Soviet Union above the Reichstag in Berlin. →

Timeline
1945 April–June

KEY:

 Europe

 Pacific

 Politics

April 12 United States
President Roosevelt dies of a brain hemorrhage; Vice President Harry S. Truman takes over as president.

April 28 Italy
Mussolini is shot dead by partisans as he tries to flee to Austria.

April 29 Italy
German forces in Italy surrender to the Allies.

April

May

April 16 Germany The Soviets attack Berlin; they vastly outnumber the Germans in troops, tanks, weapons, and aircraft.

April 30 Germany
Hitler and Eva Braun commit suicide in their bunker in Berlin.

May 2 Germany
The Reichstag falls to the Red Army after a savage three-day battle.

In February 1945, the Allies began the conquest of Germany. The British and Americans advanced from the west, while in the east, the Red Army was on the German border.

On February 8, 1945, an artillery bombardment began an attack on the Rhine River. After heavy fighting, the Allies succeeded in crossing the Rhine and establishing bridgeheads in three places.

THE BATTLE OF BERLIN, 1945

Baltic Sea

Stralsund
Rostock
Wismar
Stettin
GERMANY
Wittenberg
Küstrin
BERLIN
Frankfurt-an-der-Oder
Magdeburg
Potsdam
Beelitz
Gubin
Dessau
Elbe River
Oder River
Dresden
Bautzen Görlitz

0 40 miles
0 60 km

Key
→ Soviet attacks
———— Front line, April 16
·········· Front line, April 18
– – – Front line, May 8
------ Front line, April 25

⌃ The Red Army's capture of Berlin marks the final stages of the war.

Political Decisions

At the Yalta Conference in February 1945, the Allied politicians had agreed that the Soviet Red Army would capture Berlin. Eisenhower decided to halt at the Elbe River, about 45 miles (70 km) west of the city. There, on April 25, 1945, a US patrol met up with Soviet forces. The Allies' eastern and western advances had come together.

Timeline

January 12–17, 1945 Red Army begins advance against Germany.

February 4, 1945 Churchill, Roosevelt, and Stalin meet at Yalta to discuss postwar Europe. Germany to be divided into four administrative zones.

February 13–14, 1945 Allies bomb Dresden, killing at least 50,000 civilians.

April 16, 1945 Red Army reaches Berlin.

April 25, 1945 Red Army surrounds Berlin.

April 30, 1945 Hitler and Eva Braun commit suicide.

May 2, 1945 Berlin falls to the Soviets after three days of fierce fighting.

May 8, 1945 Victory in Europe (VE) Day; the Allies accept the surrender of Germany.

July 17–August 2, 1945 New US president Harry S. Truman and new British prime minister Clement Attlee meet Stalin at Potsdam to discuss postwar policy in Europe.

May 3 Burma
Burma surrenders to the Allies without a fight.

June 22 Okinawa Japanese resistance ends on the island of Okinawa; the battle has cost the Japanese 110,000 dead.

June

May 8 Europe Victory in Europe (VE) Day; the Allies formally accept the German surrender.

Inside Hitler's Bunker

From April 20 to April 30, 1945, Hitler lived in the Führerbunker with Eva Braun and many staff. By this time, he was a broken man. Even his closest allies began to desert him. On April 29, Hitler learned that Russian forces were close by. He married Eva Braun. The next day, the pair committed suicide. Braun took cyanide, while Hitler shot himself.

↗ Russian troops look on as the Reichstag smolders after the fall of Berlin in 1945.

The Red Army Advances

The Red Army had assembled nearly four million men for its advance into Germany. Resisting the largest single offensive of the war were four battle-weary German formations of about 600,000 men. German resistance in East Prussia soon collapsed, followed by the Hungarian capital Budapest. By April 13, the Red Army had taken the Austrian capital, Vienna.

↗ One of the last images of Hitler shows him with Hitler Youth boys in April 1945.

The Battle of Berlin

Inside Berlin, Hitler had scraped together almost every male to defend the city. The one million

Timeline
1945 July– September

July

July 17–August 2 Germany US president Harry S. Truman, Stalin, and new British prime minister Clement Attlee meet at Potsdam to discuss postwar policy in Europe.

August 6 Japan A B-29 Superfortress drops an atomic bomb on the Japanese city of Hiroshima, killing 70,000 and injuring a similar number.

August

August 9 Manchuria A huge Soviet offensive begins against the Japanese Kwantung Army.

KEY:

 Europe

Pacific

 Politics

defenders included many poorly trained members of the Volkssturm, a home guard of older men and young teenagers. Hitler himself had retreated to his bunker beneath the Chancellery, the political center of Berlin. By April 25, Berlin was surrounded. German resistance remained strong; the SS threatened to hang any man who was not fighting the Allies.

End of the Reich

By April 27, the Germans held only 15 square miles (38 sq km) of the city. Hitler ordered resistance to continue. By April 30, the Soviets had fought their way to within half a mile (800 m) of the Chancellery. Hitler married his mistress, Eva Braun, and then committed suicide.

On May 2, Berlin's commandant, Lieutenant-General Karl Weidling, surrendered. Five days later, Germany itself signed a total surrender. World War II in Europe was over.

New Yorkers celebrate Victory in Europe (VE) Day on May 8, 1945.

The Surrender

Hitler's death and the surrender of Berlin did not stop fighting in Europe. Admiral Dönitz, who now led Germany, wanted as many Germans as possible to escape, so delayed surrender as long as he could. At 2:41 A.M. on May 7, the Germans signed the surrender, which came into effect at one minute past midnight on May 9. Fighting went on until May 11 in Austria and Czechoslovakia, but the Allies could celebrate victory in Europe.

August 9 Japan An atomic bomb is dropped on Nagasaki, killing 35,000 people. The Japanese decide to surrender.

September 2 Japan Aboard the US battleship *Missouri* in Tokyo Bay, Japanese officials sign the instrument of Surrender; World War II is finally over.

September

August 15 Japan Victory over Japan (VJ) Day; the Japanese surrender is announced.

August 23 Manchuria The Soviet campaign against the Japanese ends in total victory.

Glossary

appeasement avoiding conflict by giving in to someone's demands

civil war a war between two opposing groups of citizens of the same country

commandos special forces soldiers

convoy a number of ships or vehicles traveling together

corps a military unit made up of several divisions

counterattack an attack by a defending force

destroyer a small, fast warship

division an army unit made up of 15,000 to 20,000 soldiers

evacuation the removal of people from a dangerous area

expeditionary force an army sent to serve abroad

garrison a military post

ghetto part of a city where Jews were forced to live

liberate to set free

marine a soldier based on a ship who fights on land

morale the emotional well-being of people

occupation military control of part of a country by forces from another

panzer German word for a tank

paratrooper a soldier who jumps from an aircraft with a parachute

partisan a person fighting behind enemy lines who is not a regular soldier

pocket battleship a powerful warship smaller than a battleship

Reichstag the German parliament

retaliation revenge for a previous event

strategic something that is useful in achieving a long-term goal

strategy a long-term plan of action

surrender to stop fighting and give in to the enemy

U-boat a German submarine

uprising a revolt against a ruler

"wolf pack" a group of 15 to 20 German U-boats

Further Reading

Books

Adams, Simon. *The Eastern Front* (Documenting World War II). Rosen Central, 2008.

Adams, Simon. *World War II* (Eyewitness Books). Dorling Kindersley Children, 2007.

Brinkley, Douglas. *World War II Desk Reference*. Castle Books, 2008.

Cross, Robin. *World War II*. DK Publishing, 2007.

Dickson, Keith D. *World War II for Dummies*. For Dummies, 2001.

Doeden, Matt. *Weapons of World War II*. Capstone Press, 2008.

Grant, Reg. *World War II* (DK Readers). DK CHILDREN, 2008.

Harris, Nathaniel. *World War II: Timelines*. Arcturus Publishing, 2007.

Hart, Russell, Steven Hart, and Robert John O'Neill. *World War II: Northwest Europe, 1944–1945*. Rosen Publishing Group, 2010.

Havers, Robin. *World War II: Europe, 1939–1943*. Rosen Publishing Group, 2010.

Hynson, Colin. *World War II: A Primary Source History*. Gareth Stevens Publishing, 2005.

Stolley, Richard B. *LIFE: World War II: History's Greatest Conflict in Pictures*. Bulfinch, 2005.

Ward, Geoffrey C., and Ken Burns. *The War: An Intimate History, 1941–1945*. Knopf, 2007.

Websites

www.worldwar-2.net
A complete World War II timeline, detailing events day by day.

www.secondworldwar.co.uk
A general World War II resource, including important dates, casualty figures, high commands, and trivia.

www.ibiblio.org/pha
A collection of World War II primary source materials.

www.grolier.com/wwii/ wwii_mainpage.html
The story of the war, biographies, and articles, photographs, and films.

www.war-experience.org
The Second World War Experience Center.

Index

noted
3/12/14
ML

11-11